J914.95   Day, Nancy.   •
DAY

          Your travel guide to
          ancient Greece.

D0538494

Your Travel Guide to

ANCIENT GREECE

Your Travel Guide to ANCIENT GREECE

Nancy Day

Anthony Quinn Library
3965 Cesar Chavez Ave.
Los Angeles, CA 90063
(323) 264-7715

RP RUNESTONE PRESS • MINNEAPOLIS

AN IMPRINT OF LERNER PUBLISHING GROUP

Copyright © 2001 by Nancy Day

All rights reserved. International copyright secured. No part of this book may be
reproduced, stored in a retrieval system, or transmitted in any form or by any means—
electronic, mechanical, photocopying, recording, or otherwise—without the prior
written permission of Runestone Press, except for the inclusion of brief quotations in
an acknowledged review.

Designed by: Zachary Marell and Tim Parlin
Edited by: Katy Holmgren and Martha Kranes
Illustrated by: Tim Parlin
Photo Researched by: Cheryl Hulting

Runestone Press
An imprint of Lerner Publishing Group
241 First Avenue North
Minneapolis, MN 55401 U.S.A.

Website address: www.lernerbooks.com

Library of Congress Cataloging-in-Publication Data

Day, Nancy.
    Your travel guide to ancient Greece / Nancy Day.
      p.   cm. — (Passport to history)
    Includes bibliographical references and index.
    Summary: Takes readers on a journey back in time in order to experience life in
ancient Greece, describing clothing, accommodations, foods, local customs,
transportation, a few notable personalities, and more.
    ISBN 0-8225-3076-7 (lib. bdg. : alk. paper)
    1. Greece—Guidebooks Juvenile literature. 2. Greece—Civilization—to 146 B.C.—
Juvenile literature. 3. Greece—Social life and customs Juvenile Literature.
    [1. Greece—Civilization—To 146 B.C.] I. Title. II. Series: Day, Nancy. Passport to
history.
DF78D39   2001
914.9504'76—dc21   99-36804

Manufactured in the United States of America
2 3 4 5 6 7 – JR – 06 05 04 03 02 01

CONTENTS

INTRODUCTION

GETTING STARTED

Welcome to Passport to History. You will be traveling through time and space to ancient Greece in the fifth century B.C. This travel guide will answer questions such as:

➤ **What's going on in ancient Greece?**

➤ **Which local dishes should I try?**

➤ **Who should I meet while I'm there?**

➤ **Where should I stay?**

➤ **What do I wear?**

Remember that you are going back in time to a distant culture. Some of the things that you own didn't exist during this period, which didn't have electricity. (That's why the pictures in this book are either drawings or photographs made after the invention of photography.) So forget packing your video games, hair dryers, cameras, medicines, watches, cell phones, and other modern conveniences that would make your stay in ancient Greece a lot more comfortable. But if you read this guide, you'll be able to do as the locals do—and they manage just fine, as you will see.

Like ancient Greece, modern Greece has rocky hillsides, tidy fields, and forested slopes.

NOTE TO THE TRAVELER

The ancient Greeks left literature, official documents, artworks, tools, and buildings that provide a window into their lives. Archaeologists study the remains of ancient Greek structures and examine the remains of artifacts that have survived. Historians study texts left by ancient writers, such as the ancient Greek historian Thucydides, who chronicled the Second Peloponnesian War (431–404 B.C.).

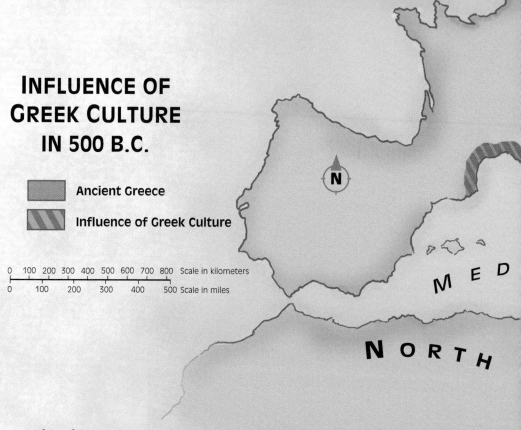

INFLUENCE OF GREEK CULTURE IN 500 B.C.

■ Ancient Greece

▨ Influence of Greek Culture

0 100 200 300 400 500 600 700 800 Scale in kilometers

0   100   200   300   400   500 Scale in miles

N

M E D

N O R T H

Archaeologists continue to uncover new clues to the culture of ancient Greece. In 1997 archaeologists conducting a dig on the location of a planned museum of modern art in Athens made a discovery. They found an ancient gymnasium, which they believe was part of a school founded by the philosopher Aristotle in 335 B.C. Just months later, the modern archaeologists stumbled upon Demosion Sima, a fifth century B.C. cemetery. Thucydides mentioned Demosion Sima in some of his writings, but historians had never known its exact location. Finds such as these answer questions about where people lived and how they spent their days.

As new discoveries are made, archaeologists and historians continue to improve their understanding of life in ancient Greece. Therefore, while this book is a good starting point for your voyage to ancient Greece, it is always possible that you will find some things to be different from what is described in this book.

WHY VISIT ANCIENT GREECE?

Check out the map. You might be surprised to see how tiny ancient Greece looks. But the region's culture has had a tremendous impact on the world. Although its influence declined after 146 B.C., when it became

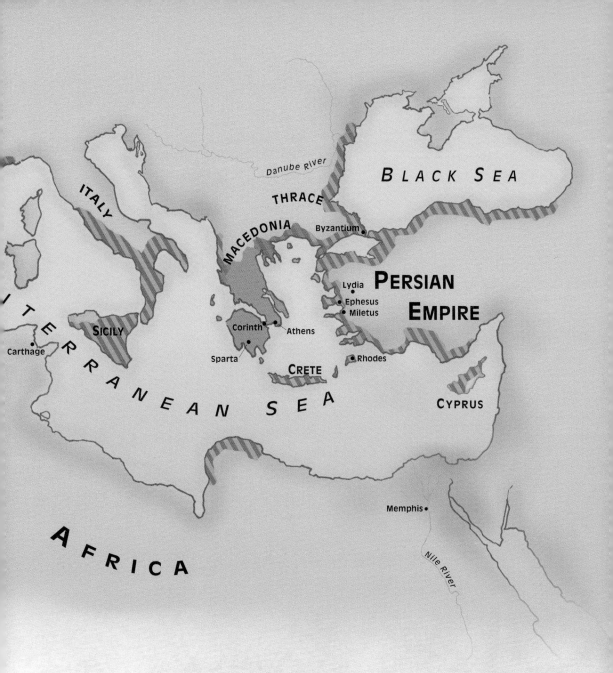

part of the Roman Empire, ancient Greece's spirit continued. Greek ideas on medicine, astronomy, and geography dominated European thought for over two thousand years. And basic concepts in architecture, art, music, mathematics, philosophy, and medicine developed by the ancient Greeks are studied in modern times.

Ancient Greece doesn't cover a lot of ground, but it does cover a lot of time. Experts trace Greek civilization back to 3000 B.C. However, the peak of Greek civilization was the fifth century (500–401) B.C. That's why this guide concentrates on fifth century B.C. Athens—the heart of ancient Greece—and its rival, Sparta.

THE BASICS

LOCATION LOWDOWN

Ancient Greece has some of the best scenery you'll find. In the southeastern corner of Europe, Greece lies on a peninsula that juts southward into the Mediterranean Sea. Snowcapped mountains, lush valleys, white limestone cliffs, and sapphire-blue water will make you wish cameras had been invented. Dolphins and porpoises frolic in the blue waters and surface into the brilliant sunshine. Deer, bears, and wolves roam the mountainsides. Swifts and eagles swoop through the sparkling air.

Inlets, harbors, bays, and gulfs crinkle ancient Greece's coast. Hundreds of islands, large and small, seem to pop up from the sea. In the southeast, the peninsula curves around a pocket of water called the Aegean Sea. A narrow strip of land connects a large area called the Peloponnesus to the mainland. Near the Peloponnesus is a peninsula called Attica. To the west, the Ionian Sea separates ancient Greece from southern Italy, which was settled by ancient Greeks.

Mountains and sea dominate the Greek landscape. But laced between the hard-to-cross mountains are narrow plains of farmland where the Greeks grow barley, wheat, grapes, and olives. Cities and villages sit on these plains.

CLIMATE

The climate in ancient Greece is Mediterranean—warm and dry. The west side of the Greek peninsula has warmer winters and more rainfall, so growing conditions are better. But most of the important cities are in the east, where weather tends to be hotter and drier. During an average

Blue waters lap at the rugged coastline of one of Greece's many islands.

year on the Attic Peninsula (where Athens is located), you'll enjoy nearly 180 sunny days and about 150 partly sunny days each year.

You may notice that it's windy. In the summer, a cool northwesterly wind (the locals call it the Etesian) blows across the Aegean Sea to Greece. Winters are relatively mild but can be quite cold and windy at times, particularly in the mountains. Icy winds, driving rain, or even snow may interfere with your plans. If possible, you should avoid the month of Lenaion (late January and early February). Its bitter north wind is powerful enough to bring down large trees.

The best time to visit ancient Greece is during the spring, summer, or fall, when many days go by without so much as a cloud in the sky. The warm weather will allow you to spend most days in the open air, which is just what the locals do.

LOCAL TIME

During your visit to ancient Greece, don't look for a clock. You can get a general idea of what time it is by using a sundial. Its gnomon (indicator) casts a shadow, which points to the time. Greek lawyers and courts often use water clocks to keep an eye on the length of speeches, which are meant to be short.

Calendars vary from one region to another. In Athens the twelve-month lunar (moon-based) calendar begins with Hekatombaion, which corresponds roughly to July. The months alternate in length between

Tech Talk

Water clocks work by allowing water to flow out slowly through a hole in the bottom of a container. The water level drops at a steady rate, so markings at measured intervals show the passage of time. An indicator (attached to a float) is sometimes used to make reading the time easier. In later years, the locals figure out how to make the dropping water level trigger bells, puppets, or even singing birds.

Sundials show ancient Greeks the time. This sundial has no gnomon (indicator).

thirty and twenty-nine days. Ancient Greeks don't date years from a fixed point like the modern calendar (which starts with one and counts years forward or backward from there). In fact, they don't have any official system for keeping track of specific years. Instead, locals may recall a prominent official or an athlete's victory at the Olympic Games. For example, you might hear about "the year Andosthenes of Arcadia won his first victory in the pankration."

THE NAME GAME

Ancient Greeks use only one name. Parents name girls after one of their grandmothers and boys after one of their grandfathers. The father's name is generally used to distinguish the boy from someone else of the same name, such as "Themistocles, son of Neocles." In some cities, such as Athens, laws discourage this practice. The citizens feel that it promotes prejudice based on a person's heritage. In these areas, a city or village name may be used instead, such as "Themistocles of Phrearrus."

You can often tell whether people are male or female just by their names. Name endings such as *-ocles, -crates, -thenes,* and *-ides* are for males. Other endings, including *-era, -ena, -dite,* and *-ima* are for females. For example, Diotima is a woman, while Diocles is a man. Names may also be chosen for their meanings, such as Xanthippe ("horse lover") or Cleopatra ("glory of her father").

New babies are named seven to ten days after birth, during which time their fathers decide whether to keep them. In Sparta state officials make this decision. Parents take unhealthy or unwanted babies outside the town to be exposed, or left outside. People rescue and raise some of the abandoned babies (often as slaves), but most die.

WHICH CITIES TO VISIT

THE CITY-STATE SYSTEM

Although we call this destination ancient Greece, the locals refer to their homeland as "Hellas" and call themselves "Hellenes." But Hellas isn't a single country with a central government. It's a region with about two hundred independent city-states. Each city-state (also called a polis) has its own government, traditions, customs, money, and army. The city-states battle with each other for land and over trade. On the other hand, they pull together to fight off invasions from the neighboring Persian Empire in 490 B.C. and 480–479 B.C.

Local pride is very strong. Natives of one city-state may be quite rude about the people of another. For example, you may overhear an Athenian refer to farmers of the neighboring Boeotia as "Boeotian pigs." And that's not a compliment.

Now Hear This
(GREEK CURSE DEPARTMENT)

May he be cast ashore, naked and stiff with cold, at Salmydessus and seized by Thracians (who will make him suffer, eating the bread of slavery), may he be covered with shellfish in the surf, may his teeth chatter like a dog's, as he lies face downwards by the margin of the waves.

—*Archilochus, first part of the seventh century* B.C.

Temples made of gleaming white marble top the Acropolis, a rocky hill in the heart of Athens.

Out-of-town travelers who need help can consult their *proxenos,* a sort of embassy representative. The proxenos lives in one polis, but he represents the interests of another. A citizen of Thebes visiting Athens might see the Theban proxenos to get a loan, to get help with a legal problem, or to get tickets to the theater.

ANCIENT GREECE IN 440 B.C.

N

IONIAN SEA

AEGEAN SEA

PERSIAN

Delphi

Boeotia

Thebes

Corinth

Attica

Athens

Olympia

Peloponnesus

Sparta

EMPIRE

▇ Athenian Empire

▇ Spartan Allies

| 0 | 100 | Scale in kilometers |
| 0 | 50 | 100 | Scale in miles |

CRETE

ATHENS

When you arrive in Athens, you will be surprised by the extraordinary contrast between dazzling beauty and revolting filth. The streets are full of people who range from proud, wealthy citizens with slaves to pitiful creatures with bodies disfigured by war or untreated disease.

Above all, you will notice the stench. With no sewers or trash collection, waste piles up in the narrow streets and winding alleys of Athens. The Eridanus, a river that runs through the heart of the city, is a dumping ground for garbage.

On the other hand, the beauty of Athens is truly awesome. Stately, painted columns surround spectacular temples. Statues of exquisite artistry line the courtyards and pathways. Outside the city gates lie tombs with carved marble figures or scenes. Other tombs have simple jars, beautiful in shape and design.

Above the roofs of the town is the majestic Acropolis—a rocky, flat-topped hill that towers over the city. Houses and other buildings cluster around the base of the Acropolis. Perched on top are spectacular temples, such as the Parthenon, that look dazzling in the crisp, clear air.

At the foot of the Acropolis, you'll find the Agora. A large open-air market and public meeting place, the Agora is surrounded by long, spacious porticoes (covered porches with columns). Lively painted scenes decorate the walls. The Agora is a great place to hang out, eat, shop, and talk to the locals. You'll want to come here more than once, so be sure to mark your map!

SPARTA

In the Peloponnesus, you'll find Sparta, one of the most powerful city-states of mainland Greece. Sparta lies in a valley along a series of low hills overlooking the river Eurotas. It will look more like a cluster of small villages than a city. Spartans dislike wealth and pomp, and they build few public stone monuments. There is an acropolis with a few temples, including one dedicated to the goddess Athena. As in Athens, an agora spreads at its base.

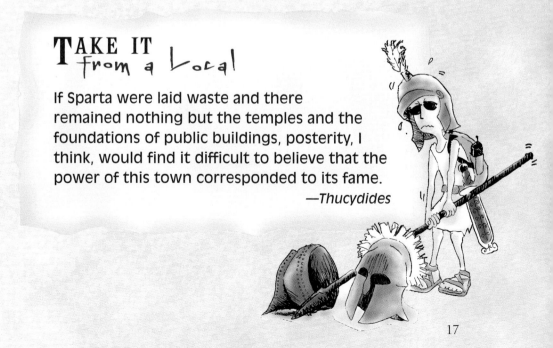

TAKE IT from a Local

If Sparta were laid waste and there remained nothing but the temples and the foundations of public buildings, posterity, I think, would find it difficult to believe that the power of this town corresponded to its fame.

—*Thucydides*

MONEY MATTERS

Ancient Greeks use beautiful coins and plain iron oboloi as money. Each Greek city-state uses a different form of currency. Spartans pay for goods with oboloi, or rods (on right), *while Athenians use a variety of different coins.*

AN OBOL FOR YOUR THOUGHTS

Ancient Greek money may seem a little confusing at first. If you arrive before the 600s B.C., you will find no money at all. The only way to buy things is to trade for them.

Ancient Greeks shape copper ingots (bars) like these into jewelry. They also trade ingots for other items.

Later on, you may find bars of silver, called ingots, in circulation. Several ingots make up one talent. One talent equals almost fifty eight-pounds of silver. As you might expect, talents are hard to lug around while you're sightseeing. You may spot iron rods, called oboloi, traded by the drachma (an amount approximating a handful). Six oboloi equal one drachma. Throughout the 500s B.C., you will run into oboloi across all of Greece. In the 400s B.C., you will find them only in Sparta.

After 500 B.C., each Greek city-state mints (makes) its own coins in whatever values that it pleases. Ancient Greeks made the earliest coins out of electrum, a natural combination of gold and silver. But most coins you will see are solid silver. A few are made of gold. In fifth-century Athens, the coins most often used are drachmae and oboloi. These coins have the value of the older drachmae and oboloi.

Hot Hint

Don't bother trying to pass off currency from home. Modern coins contain little or no precious metal. That means the coins are worthless as far as the locals are concerned. And paper money hasn't even been invented yet!

Be advised that in outlying areas you may encounter some unusual forms of currency. So many squid swim in the waters off Eretria that the townspeople use the sea creatures for currency—it's easier than minting coins. But be forewarned. The slimy little critters make a mess out of your wallet. And good luck getting rid of that smell!

The Athenian owl coin features the head of the goddess Athena on one side and an owl on the other.

WHERE TO FIND MONEY

Athenian owls, or glaux (coins showing the head of Athena on the front and an owl on the back), are good across ancient Greece. But most Greek coins can be used only in their home city-state. This can complicate traveling from one area to another.

You'll want to seek out money changers, who exchange foreign currency for local coins. Look for money changers in the agoras. For their services, of course, they charge a fee.

Greek coins contain an amount of precious metal worth their face value. The money changer will weigh your coins and then determine whether the metal is genuine.

If you really find yourself short of money, you can borrow some from a money lender. However, this can be expensive. The interest rate on loans often runs as high as 12 to 18 percent. Interest can be even higher for riskier loans. Money for a dangerous sea voyage, for example, may be loaned at 24 percent interest. If you decide to borrow money, you'll be asked to sign a receipt in front of witnesses and to give a pledge of a handshake. Or you may be asked to sign a bond (a document promising repayment).

Prices
OF COMMON GOODS

1 loaf of bread—1 obol

1 lamb—8 drachmae

1 sheep—10 to 20 drachmae

1 ox—up to 100 drachmae

1 amphoreus (large container) of high-quality wine—20 drachmae

1 pair of shoes, unless highly decorated—2 drachmae

1 small house—700 drachmae

Average Athenian's pay for one day of work—1½ to 2 drachmae

Unskilled laborer's pay for one day of work—3 oboloi

HOW TO GET AROUND

BY LAND

Travel in ancient Greece can be tricky, even within a single city. Houses aren't numbered or identified in any way, and many streets don't have names. The locals either know where they are going or send a slave ahead to find out. But don't let that stop you from exploring as much of the cities as time allows.

To travel to inland sites, you must go by land. But keep in mind that in this mountainous region, overland travel can be difficult. To go long distances, rich travelers ride horses, while the poor ride donkeys. Saddles and stirrups haven't been invented yet, so many locals find riding very uncomfortable. For shorter trips, ancient Greeks sometimes ride in

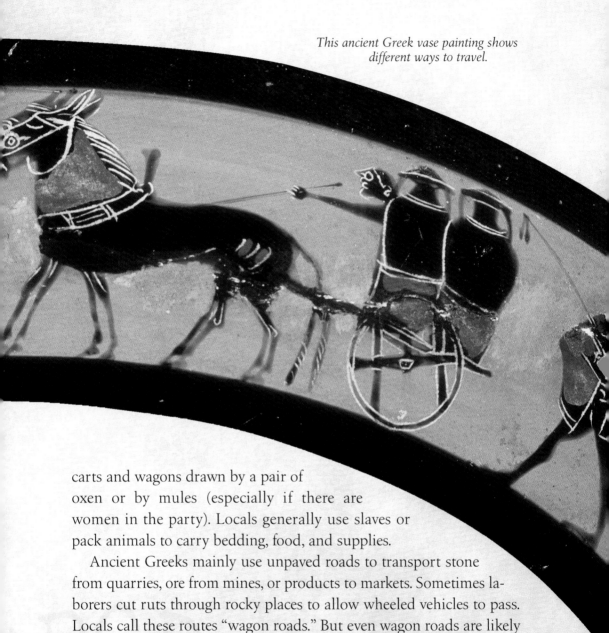

This ancient Greek vase painting shows different ways to travel.

carts and wagons drawn by a pair of oxen or by mules (especially if there are women in the party). Locals generally use slaves or pack animals to carry bedding, food, and supplies.

Ancient Greeks mainly use unpaved roads to transport stone from quarries, ore from mines, or products to markets. Sometimes laborers cut ruts through rocky places to allow wheeled vehicles to pass. Locals call these routes "wagon roads." But even wagon roads are likely to have stones and deep, irregular gullies (trenches caused by heavy rains). In dry spots, dust can lie many inches deep.

It's often just as fast to walk. But be forewarned—you won't find any sidewalks for people on foot. If you meet a large wagon or a herd of cattle, you'll be forced to stand aside or even climb up a wall for safety. If

you don't have any luggage, you will make better time by cutting across hills and mountains on footpaths. Even so, a journey from Athens to Delphi, for example, will take many days of walking.

Occasionally, you will come to streams that must be crossed. Look for a ford (a shallow area where you can wade across). If you don't find a ford, look for someone to ferry you on a small boat or raft.

BY WATER

Travel by ship is much more convenient and comfortable than travel overland. And luckily many places you'll want to visit in ancient Greece lie on or near the coast. As the Athenian philosopher Plato points out, most city-states cluster around the water "like frogs on a pond." The sea also provides a way to reach the many Greek islands and areas outside ancient Greece. Whenever possible, the ship will stay close to shore in case of sudden storms or pirate attacks. Ships sail only during daylight,

This relief from the fourth century B.C. shows a Greek horseman.

stopping each night to anchor.

Trade—in food and goods—is the main reason for travel between the Greek mainland and the islands. But locals may travel by ship to take part in games and festivals in other city-states. Most locals are reluctant travelers. Sick people, however, may take great risks in order to reach temples where they hope to be cured by Asclepius, the god of healing.

IMPORTANT
Safety Tip

If you find a bridge, take a good look before you cross it. The Greeks don't like changing nature or going against the will of the gods. So they build rickety wooden bridges that the river can easily demolish.

This vase shows ancient Greek farmers, who sell their goods in cities. Many farmers rent farms from rich landowners.

LOCAL CUSTOMS & MANNERS

WHAT YOU CAN EXPECT FROM THE LOCALS

Ancient Greeks pride themselves on their hospitality. They are quite hungry for news, particularly from foreign parts (although they may not believe just how foreign you are). On the other hand, they consider anyone who does not speak Greek to be uncivilized. To them, strangers (including you) are barbarians.

Keep in mind that foreigners aren't allowed to take part in public life. Even *metics* (Greeks who leave their home city-state permanently to live and work in another Greek city) may not vote, own land, or own houses in their adopted polis. Metics pay extra taxes and have many citizen's duties (such as military service). But they cannot become citizens. In fact, Sparta discourages foreign settlers. Periodic purges called *xenelasia* expel (get rid of) foreign residents.

Back TO THE FUTURE

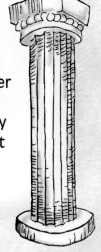

Although the locals all speak Greek, different dialects (versions of the language) are spoken in various regions. You may not be able to hear the differences. But the locals can tell by accents and unusual words whether someone is from Athens, Sparta, or another area. And keep in mind that the modern-day language known as Greek is very different from its ancestor. Languages change and evolve over time, and ancient Greek was spoken a long time ago!

DEMOCRACY RULES

Ancient Greece is famous for being the seat of democracy. But it has less in common with modern-day democratic governments than you might expect. Ancient Greeks love to talk politics, so you'll probably want to know a little bit about how their government really does work. Here's a quick overview.

Kings once ruled Athens. When you visit, you'll find the city governed by archons, who are sort of like chief executives. The archons are elected by the Assembly, which is made up of citizens (city-state residents with full rights). The Assembly makes laws, raises taxes, determines how the government will spend money, and establishes foreign policy. Every citizen has a direct say in the government through his vote in the Assembly.

The catch is that not everyone can be a citizen. Slaves, women, and people under age eighteen cannot be citizens. Neither can men whose fathers weren't born in Athens. Nevertheless, here you see the beginnings of democracy—the form of government in which citizens vote on public matters.

Five hundred citizens make up the Council, which meets almost every day to conduct routine business. They oversee candidates for elections, supervise officials, manage finances, and handle foreign affairs. Fifty members of the Council serve on the executive committee, which is on call for matters that come up between Council meetings.

TAKE IT from a Local

Our constitution is called a democracy because power is in the hands not of a minority but of the whole people.

—Pericles, funeral oration during the Peloponnesian War, winter of 431–430 B.C.

Sparta is ruled by two elected kings. Five ephors (officials) are elected every year. The ephors have the power to fire a king for misconduct. The two kings and twenty-eight male citizens over the age of sixty (when Spartan men retire from the military) form a Council of Elders. All citizens belong to the Assembly. The Council of Elders and the Assembly work together to govern Sparta. This government is very stable.

In Sparta, citizens are called Spartiates or *homoioi*. They are men whose families have lived in Sparta for generations. Citizens may own property, vote, serve in the army, and participate in the government. *Perioikoi*, or "dwellers around or about," can own property and handle most trade and commerce in Sparta, but they cannot vote.

Sparta was nearly destroyed by the revolt of the Messenians, a people the Spartans had conquered in the eighth century B.C. during the Messenian War. After they put down the rebellion, the Spartans set up a system to tightly control the population. The Spartans forced the Messenians to be *helots*, or serfs. The helots work small plots of land on estates owned by Spartan citizens and must turn over part of what they produce to the owner.

THE SOCIAL SCENE

The ancient Greeks divide the free population into classes. If a father is a citizen, his son is also a citizen. Most citizens aren't rich or powerful, but they do have rights. Many city-states have free noncitizens and serfs. Some serfs, such as the helots, labor long and hard for very little. The people with the fewest rights are slaves.

You will also find that kinship groups are important. Every male citizen belongs to a *phratriai*, a brotherhood that orders his religious and social life. Within each phratriai is at least one *genos*, an aristocratic family who claims a common ancestor, often a god or hero from Greek mythology. Membership in a phratriai passes from father to son.

Women have few rights. They can't be citizens. Laws forbid Athenian women to own much property, to inherit in their own names, to vote, or to attend the Assembly. An ancient Greek woman is in the care of her father, husband, or a male guardian for her whole life. The man conducts all her business. He even arranges her marriage.

Ancient Greeks feel that a woman's most important role is motherhood. Very few skilled or well-paying trades are open to women. In fact, the locals look down on men whose wives must work. You may find female innkeepers (usually metics). Some women work as nurses and midwives. Poor women, often widows, may have lowly jobs such as street cleaning. And you may spot some women selling goods in the market or working alongside their husbands. The most important public role a woman can have is as a priestess.

Women take part in some public religious festivals. But most of the time, Greek women stay at home. Greek husbands consider it honorable to shield their wives from public view by having separate sections in their homes for women. Women spend most of their time in the women's quarters of the house, where they spin, weave, look after children, and supervise slaves. Spartan women have more freedom than women in other parts of Greece. Women of the Spartiate class can be outdoors freely. They can gain property through dowries (bridal money) and inheritances. By the fourth century B.C., women own nearly two-fifths of the land in Sparta.

This painting of an ancient Greek woman shows her holding a spindle, a stick used in spinning thread.

30

A female slave (at right) *helps her mistress pick a piece of jewelry.*

SLAVERY

Don't be surprised to see slaves in Athens and across Greece. Everyone who isn't very poor owns at least one slave. Most citizens in Athens own two or three slaves, but wealthy men may own ten, twenty, or more. In the late fifth century B.C., Nicias, one of the city-state's richest men, owns one thousand slaves. He has so many that he rents them out to fellow citizens for one obol a slave per day.

Some slaves are born into slavery. Professional kidnappers take some from non-Greek-speaking regions surrounding Greece, such as Thrace. Sometimes prisoners of war become slaves. In wartime Greeks even enslave fellow Greeks (especially women and children, who make useful house slaves).

Slaves perform a variety of jobs in ancient Greece. They help run households, work in mines, do manufacturing work, labor on farms, or assist their masters with their craft or trade. Slaves called pedagogues accompany wealthy boys to school to make sure that they learn properly. Some slaves are owned by the state and work as jury clerks, coin

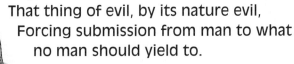

TAKE IT from a Local

> Slavery,
> That thing of evil, by its nature evil,
> Forcing submission from man to what
> no man should yield to.
> —*the playwright Euripides*

testers, and even executioners. Shopkeepers and artisans train slaves to help with their businesses.

The worst place for a slave is in the silver mines of Lávrion. Slaves go into the mineshafts nearly naked and shackled in chains. They carry oil-burning lamps as their only source of light. The slaves crawl or lie in tunnels only two or three feet high and about the same width, working a ten-hour shift. The work is dangerous and exhausting. Many die under the harsh conditions. Masters send down groups of slaves in shifts, so digging continues night and day.

Treatment of slaves varies. Some owners pay slaves for their work, and owners may free slaves after a period of service. If a trial needs a slave's testimony,

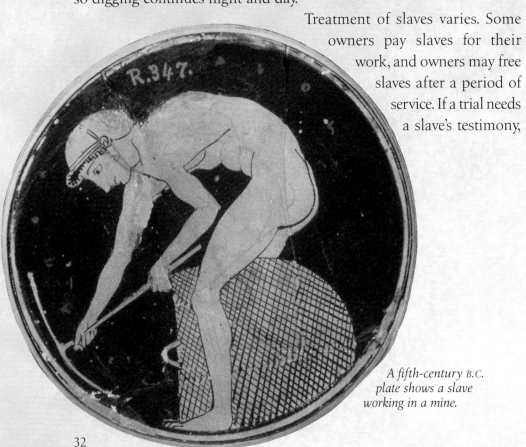

A fifth-century B.C. plate shows a slave working in a mine.

the court assumes the slave is loyal to the master. The slave is tortured to make sure he or she tells the truth. Slaves who steal or try to escape may be whipped, placed in the pillory (a wooden frame to hold the head and hands), or branded (permanently marked by burning).

You'll see that few locals find any problem with the idea of slavery. In fact, in the 300s B.C., the Greek philosopher Aristotle says that certain men become slaves because they are naturally obedient. Euripides, a Greek playwright in the 400s B.C., feels differently.

From Dawn to Dusk

The ancient Greek's day begins at dawn or even earlier, so don't plan on sleeping in. Oil lamps are a poor substitute for sunlight, and few locals can afford to waste the free sunshine. So at the first sign of daybreak, the locals roll out of bed and start their day.

After lunch, some Greeks enjoy a nap. By the 400s B.C., the community-wide nap has fallen out of favor. It seems that enemies captured a Greek town by a surprise attack while all the residents napped. The locals decided that it is not a very good idea for everyone to rest at the same time.

Don't figure on staying up late—Greeks go to bed early. Interlaced cords or leather thongs stretched between wooden bedframes support mattresses.

Tech Talk

Lamps are usually made from pottery (although you may see some stone or bronze lamps). They have two openings—one for filling the lamp with olive oil, which serves as the fuel, the other for inserting the wick. To light the wick, use sparks from the glowing embers of the fireplace or rub two sticks together until you make fire. The olive oil will keep the wick fueled for hours.

LOCAL MANNERS

Mind your manners while visiting ancient Greece. As you travel, walk at a dignified pace. Rushing is rude. Boys should rise when an older man enters the room and should stand up straight. Don't giggle, grab at something on the dinner table, or sit with your legs crossed.

In Athens local men often ask guests to dinner. The invitation will come only a day or two ahead of time, or perhaps even on the same day. It will be a verbal invitation, not written, and may come through a friend or a slave.

At the entrance to the house, you may see written above the door, "Let no evil enter here." If there is no metal knocker, beat on the door and call *"Pai!"* ("Boy!"). A household slave or a foreign-born porter will greet you. Be sure to enter right foot first—the ancient Greeks consider it bad luck to cross a threshold with the left.

Don't shake your host's hand—that's only for sealing formal agreements. Don't bow either. People who aren't slaves bow only when making an offering to the gods or acknowledging an omen (sign). And only family members or very close friends exchange kisses and hugs.

Handy WORDS & PHRASES

If you meet someone you know on the street, use the handy word *chaire*, which means both "hail" and "farewell."

LOCAL BELIEFS

Ancient Greeks believe in many gods, all descendants of Gaia (the Earth) and Uranos (the sky). Twelve major gods and goddesses, known as the Olympian gods, are believed to live on Mount Olympus. Among these are Poseidon, god of the sea, and Demeter, goddess of grain crops. Zeus, he father of all gods and mortals, rules the heavens. Artemis is the goddess of the moon, while her brother Apollo is the god of the sun. Athena is the goddess of wisdom and of war.

A second important group of gods, the Chthonians, are gods of the earth and the underworld. Lesser gods, called demigods, and heroes also play roles in Greek religion. Like ordinary people, the gods fall in love, marry, have children, and fight. But the gods are stronger, cleverer, braver, and immortal.

The locals rely on the gods to settle problems, explain the universe, and provide help on any occasion. They believe that the gods make the crops sprout, determine who wins wars, and cause epidemics of disease. Hoping to influence the gods, the Greeks (the city-state government as well as individuals) offer the gods prayers and sacrifices (offerings include crops or ritually killed animals).

Ancient Greeks build temples to be the houses of the gods. The people build beautiful structures to honor the gods, but the temples don't seat worshipers. If you wish to attend religious ceremonies, go to the altars outside of the temples. Priests and priestesses will hold a ceremony there. Although locals attend these public events, most people also worship at home altars, where they offer sacrifices to the gods.

Inside the temples, priests and priestesses perform only special religious services to help the city-state. Priests and priestesses also purify houses after a birth or death, lead weddings and funerals, conduct sacrifices, participate in festivals, and look after sacred objects stored in the temples.

In modern times, this statue of Zeus is in the Vatican Museum in Vatican City in Rome, Italy.

The ancient Greeks also believe that the gods reveal their wishes in mysterious signs. *Mantis*, or seers, understand these signs from the gods. Seers observe the way animals act, such as the way that a passing bird flies or sounds. A significant action will help to predict the future. Seers also examine the organs, particularly the liver, of sacrificed animals. A healthy-looking liver means that the gods approve. An unhealthy liver is a sign of disapproval.

You may want to try an interesting rite known as *kledon*. Worshipers practice kledon at temples of the god Hermes, a messenger of the gods. Whisper a question into the ear of the god's statue. Then immediately plug your ears and leave the temple. Outside, when you get beyond the town marketplace, unplug your ears and listen for the god's answer in the conversations of people walking by.

Ancient Greeks try to predict events in other ways, too. Many people place great meaning on omens, events believed to signal good or bad luck. People consider a sneeze to be a good omen about whatever is being discussed or thought of at that moment. A storm when a ship sets sail is a bad omen.

SIDE TRIP TRIVIA

If you stop by India in the 500s B.C., you will find an explosion of new ideas, philosophies, and beliefs. Siddhartha Gautama, better known as the "Buddha," or "Enlightened One," is born in northern India around 560 B.C. He is the founder of Buddhism. Another major world religion, Hinduism, is getting its start in India during this period as well.

A Greek painting shows mourners paying their last respects to the dead.

DEATH & BEYOND

Many Greeks believe in some form of life after death. Some believe that the dead live on in their tombs. Others believe in an underworld, a cold and gloomy place where souls remain for a bleak eternity. In the sixth century B.C., people start to believe that a nice underworld awaits those who are good in life.

When someone dies, the women of the family take care of the body. They wash it and anoint it with oil, then dress it in white robes. They put a coin in the dead person's mouth. (Ancient Greeks believe that the dead must pay the mythical ferryman Charon. He takes souls across the mythical river Styx to the underworld.) Then the family puts the body on display for relatives and friends. In a cemetery outside the city, they will bury the remains and some of the dead person's possessions. According to ancient Greek belief, the unburied dead can't enter the underworld. So the Greeks pitch the bodies of executed criminals into the sea or into open pits. After people take part in the funeral, they must purify themselves by washing. Priests don't attend at all.

WHAT TO WEAR

CLOTHES

Simple, loose-fitting clothes are comfortable in Greece's hot climate. The basic outfit for men and women is a tunic made from a square of wool or linen loosely draped around the body and pinned together. The tunic looks like a sleeveless nightgown or dress.

A woman's tunic, called a *peplos*, typically falls to her feet. Wearers pin extra material around the shoulders and might add a belt. Outside the house, a woman always wears a cloak. A man's tunic is called a *chiton*. The long version falls to the feet, while a shorter version falls to the knees. Workmen and farmers usually pick the shorter chiton. Soldiers wear short chitons under their body armor.

Most of the time, men wear few clothes or none at all. Yes, that's none. They feel that nakedness is just more practical for sports, swimming, and working in hot weather or in hot places, such as a potter's kiln room. When women are around, men put on their chitons. Throughout most of Greece, women and girls always wear clothes. But in Sparta, girls exercise and play sports wearing little or no clothing.

You'll see wealthy people in expensive, brightly colored clothes. Ancient Greeks make dyes from plants and animals. For example, purple comes from sea snails. Workers use an insect larva to make a violet dye.

This ancient Greek woman holds a mirror and a box for makeup or jewelry. Her fancy peplos *is carefully draped.*

Hot Hint

Greeks feel that it is shameful
for women to cut their hair.
Female visitors who have
short hair may want to cover it
with a scarf to avoid stares.

Most of the time, people go barefoot, so you won't need to pack a lot of shoes. Men do wear leather boots when they walk or ride in the country. And on very rough ground, men wear leather sandals polished with olive oil. Cork soles make shoes more comfortable. Women sometimes wear simple red or yellow leather sandals.

HAIR

Women wear their hair long and have various ways of styling it. Young, unmarried women let their hair flow over their shoulders, but older women often cover their hair with a scarf and sometimes add a veil.

As you walk around town, you'll see barbershops in the street-side walls of some of the houses. Local men spend a lot of time at the barbershop because they find some of the best gossip there.

Men wear their hair in many different styles. Some roll up long hair and tuck it into a headband or twist it into two braids and wrap it around their heads. Others wear their hair short. They also comb, oil, and trim their beards with care. Beards are considered manly. Spartan warriors are famous for their long curls.

BEAUTY

Wealthy women use hair combs, perfume, and makeup. They have a round flat pot called a *pyxis* to hold their perfumes and makeup. Women use white lead to lighten their skin and alkanet root to redden their cheeks. They consider a suntan unattractive. When outdoors they

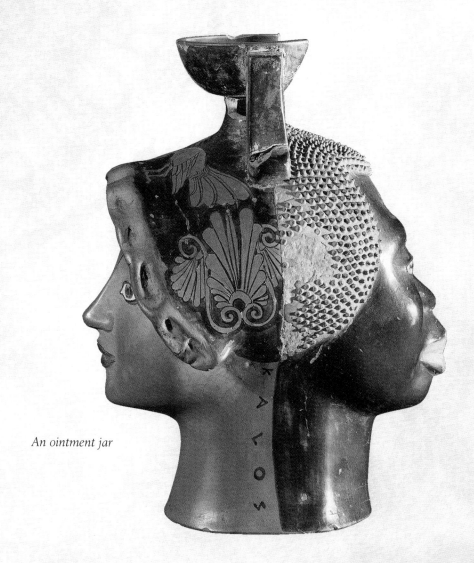

An ointment jar

wear a hat, pull their cloak up over their head, or wear a veil called a *kredemnon*. They may also have slaves hold parasols (umbrellas) for shade.

Many women have pierced ears. They also wear necklaces, bracelets, and anklets. They carry fans made of thin light wood or peacock feathers.

Greek men of earlier periods wore a lot of jewelry. By the fourth and fifth centuries B.C., most men have given it up. In fact, if you are male and are wearing an earring, you will surely be spotted as a foreigner. A man may choose to wear a signet ring, which has a design, name, or initials carved on its surface. The locals seal documents and containers by pressing the signet ring against soft clay to leave a stamped image.

WHAT TO SEE & DO

The Parthenon is one of Athens's most majestic buildings. In ancient times, much of the Parthenon is brightly painted.

SITES TO SEE

The Parthenon If you visit Athens after 432 B.C., you won't be able to miss the most glorious building of the ancient world—the Parthenon. You can see it from miles away, even from the sea. Reach it by walking up the Panathenaic Way, a special road leading from the Agora to the Acropolis.

Back TO THE FUTURE

The art and architecture of ancient Greece will influence art and architecture many years into the future—just look at many of the government buildings in Washington, D.C.

The Parthenon is the centerpiece of a magnificent collection of temples and monuments built in the second half of the 400s B.C. The spiritual center of Athens, the Parthenon is the temple of Athena, the guardian goddess of Athens.

Sculptures and many parts of the marble building are brightly painted. The design of the Parthenon demonstrates the ancient Greek values of harmony and proportion. Subtle curves correct an optical illusion of sagging that a straight line can give. The columns lean slightly inward so that they look perfectly straight. And check out the sculpted figures high on the outside wall. The beautifully carved and colorfully painted human and animal figures depict a religious procession called the Panathenaia.

The Temple of the Delphic Oracle Delphi, in central Greece, is the sanctuary (sacred location) of the god Apollo. A temple there contains the Delphic Oracle, the most famous of the Greek world's oracles (priestly fortune-tellers). The Delphic Oracle is a priestess called the Pythia. You can seek advice from her on personal matters, such as marriage, health, or business. Representatives of city governments come to ask questions of public importance.

If you choose to visit the oracle, you'll undergo a ritual purification (cleansing ceremony) before you see the Pythia in the temple's sanctum (inner room). You'll find her sitting on a three-legged stool. When you ask your question, she'll go into a trance to speak Apollo's answer.

Lush greenery at Delphi

Don't be surprised if you don't understand what she says. The Pythia delivers the god's answer in garbled form. A priest will interpret the answer, often speaking in verse. You will be expected to leave a valuable gift for this service.

Olympia Olympia is a sanctuary and sports complex sacred to the god Zeus. Although Olympia is known mainly as the site of the Olympic Games, you may want to visit even when the Games are not being held. Although at times it contains bathhouses, restaurants, a meeting hall, and many other amenities, it has no permanent residents or government.

The heart of Olympia is the walled sacred area that houses a magnificent forty-foot-tall gold and ivory statue of Zeus. If you hear anyone complain (as one Greek did) that Zeus's head is so close to the roof beams that he couldn't possibly stand up, remember that there's a complainer in every crowd. Ancient people consider the statue one of the seven wonders of the world.

The Assembly If you want to observe the Assembly of Athens (you will not be allowed to vote, of course), go to the open-air theater on the Pnyx hill just after dawn. At least five thousand citizens will be present. If attendance is low, officials carrying a rope dipped in red dye go out into the streets to round up the slackers. Stay out of their way. Anyone found with a red stain on his cloak is fined.

To start the Assembly, the town crier calls for silence. Priests sacrifice pigs and, with the blood, draw a sacred circle around the Assembly. If there is a bad omen (whether it's an earthquake or just a passing rain shower), the meeting will be called off.

"Who wishes to speak?" the crier asks, and a speaker then mounts the platform. During the speeches, people from opposing political groups sling insults and try to out-shout each other. The crowd whistles and stamps their feet. A famous orator (speaker) named Demosthenes taught himself to speak over this noise. He went to the seashore and yelled against the sound of waves to make himself heard.

A bust of Demosthenes

SCHOOL

School in ancient Greece is a lot different than school in modern times. In Athens you will find that schooling usually begins at age seven and lasts about ten years. But not everyone gets an education. Poor children do not go to school at all. Lower-income boys leave after three or four years. At age eighteen, a boy becomes known as an *ephebos* (youth) and begins two years of military training. After that, a rich young man may go back to school.

You won't find any girls in school. Mothers teach their daughters at home. The girls learn to spin, weave, and look after the house. Only a few wealthy girls learn to read and write (they are taught at home by an educated slave). Sparta is the only place in ancient Greece where women go to school by law. The focus is on rigorous physical training to keep them fit for bearing babies. Teachers also train Spartan girls in the skills for religious festivals—choral singing, dancing, and gymnastics.

If you spend a day at school, you will find three types of teachers. *Paidotribes* (coaches) teach sports. Wrestling and gymnastics are considered the most important. *Kitharistes* teach music, especially singing and playing the lyre for poetry recitations. All schoolboys learn to play a musical instrument, such as the lyre, the kithara, or the double pipes.

The *grammatistes* teach reading, writing, arithmetic, and literature. Students memorize poetry written by respected writers. The local kids will amaze you with their ability to recite long passages. Students write on a wax-coated tablet made of wood. They scratch it with the sharp point of a tool called a stylus. Using the flat end, they can smooth out any mistakes. People save papyrus, the only paperlike material they have, for important documents such as death certificates, tax records, and works of literature. There are no calculators or computers, but you can use an abacus (a counting device) for math.

Sparta is famous for its program of military training. At age seven, all boys leave home to be brought up in packs under the supervision of older boys, who report to a state officer. By age twelve, the boys live in barracks. They sleep on mattresses made of river rushes that they must gather themselves. Even in winter, they're allowed only one outer garment and no shoes. Their diet consists only of bad-tasting black broth, but they are encouraged to steal additional food. If the boys are found out, authorities beat them—not for stealing but for getting caught.

But you don't need to be at school to learn in ancient Greece. Keep in mind that one of the greatest things about ancient Greece is that everywhere you'll meet people who want to talk about all kinds of things. Thinking and sharing ideas is a major part of Greek life (for wealthy men at least).

If you want a real challenge, seek out Socrates (look for him at the Agora in Athens in the late 400s B.C.). He is easy to spot in this country that prizes perfectly sculpted bodies—he is fat, pot-bellied, bald-headed, and waddles like a duck (and that's how his friends describe him!). His appearance hides a kind heart and one of the greatest minds in history.

Young boys in ancient Greece learn musical skills from their kitharistes.

Socrates develops a teaching style called the Socratic method. He uses a stream of questions to get answers that lead to a universal truth. He is especially fond of exposing ignorance in people who consider themselves experts. And he likes to make people think about what their statements really mean. He wanders the Agora looking for a challenging conversation. If you talk with him, he will probably start by getting you to say something obvious, such as, "Truth is good." Then he will get you to agree that if what you said is true, then certainly this must be true: "Truth is not telling lies."

"If that is true," he will continue, "then you must agree that this must be true: Vicious dogs don't tell lies. So it follows that vicious dogs are good." In a few sentences, he will have you so confused that you may simply walk away shaking your head.

This procession of water carriers is part of the Panathenaia.

SPECIAL EVENTS

Panathenaia The largest and best of the festivals (other than the Olympic Games) is the Panathenaia, where Athenians honor the goddess Athena. It is held on the twenty-eighth of Hekatombaion, the first month of each year. (The ancient Greeks began their year in the summer.) But the Great Panathenaia, held each fourth year, is particularly spectacular.

(Facing page) *A sacrifice is an important part of many festivals in ancient Greece.*

The high point of the Panathenaia is the procession to the Acropolis. The first thing you'll see is a huge ship on wheels. Look carefully at the brightly colored "sail." It is actually a sacred robe, a gift to Athena. It will be presented to the magnificent statue of the goddess Athena in the Parthenon. Each year, priests supervise specially chosen Athenian girls who weave the goddess a new robe. It will be laid on the statue's knees as an offering.

After the ship, you will see girls carrying wine jars and baskets of perfume. Stand back a little bit—next in line will be bulls to be sacrificed. A group of men in red cloaks will follow. These men are the metics, who are included in the procession to symbolize the Athenians' hope for a united Greece. Following them you'll see young men bearing jars, old men with olive branches, and a group of chariots pulled by horses. At the end of the procession is a group of youths on horseback. Soldiers, on foot and on horseback, are also a large part of the procession.

If you enjoy marching in parades, feel free to join in. Even freed slaves walk in the procession carrying branches from oak trees. The idea is to represent all classes of Athenians.

Festivals Galore Look for local festivals wherever you travel. Athens alone has about 150 festivals a year. In Pyanopsion (October), check out a special three-day women's festival, Thesmophoria, which honors the goddess Demeter. You will find shelters to camp in, but only women are allowed to attend.

The Brauronia is held in the month of Munichion (April) in Brauron, a town in Attica. The Brauronia honors the goddess Artemis. Little girls dress up like bears and are called bears by the locals. The girls offer various bear-shaped objects to the goddess.

The Gymnopaidiai is the "Festival of the Naked Youths." It is held in Sparta in Hekatombaion (July). It features several days of gymnastic displays and dancing by boys and men. The locals sing hymns to the gods and to Spartan heroes.

The Dionysia, the festival of Dionysus, the god of wine, is held in Elaphebolion (March). During the festival, plays are performed in the Theater of Dionysus in Athens. People from all over Athens and the outlying areas come to the festival, which opens with a day of sacrifices, processions, and worship. By sunrise on the second day, the theater will be packed with people waiting for the plays to begin.

Theater Going to a play is a normal part of Greek life. Everyone (except slaves and sometimes women) is encouraged to attend.

Get an early start—the seats fill up before dawn. The plays are held in amphitheaters, or large, open-air theaters shaped like half-circles

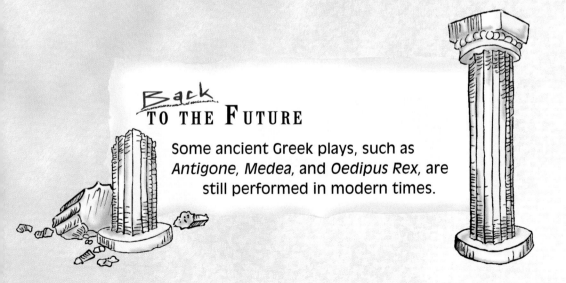

BACK TO THE FUTURE

Some ancient Greek plays, such as *Antigone*, *Medea*, and *Oedipus Rex*, are still performed in modern times.

Greek actors wear exaggerated masks to assume their characters' identities.

around a stage. About fifty rows of wood or stone benches rise away from the stage on a slope. The seats are hard, so bring a cushion (that's what the locals do). Markings on the bench show how much room to take.

You will be surprised that you can hear every word spoken on the stage, even from the back row. Be prepared to settle in—the performance may last all day. A single day's performances may include three complete tragedies, a comedy, and a satyr play (a play in which actors wear horses' tails and ears).

In the fifth century B.C., plays feature individual actors, as well as a chorus, to tell the story of the play. And all of the actors speak or sing the dialogue in verse.

Men play all the parts, even the female ones. The actors wear stiffened linen or clay masks, which they change to move from one role to another. The large mouths of the masks work like megaphones to help make the voices louder. The platform shoes, the headdresses, and the expressions on the masks make the actors visible to the back of the theater. You won't see many special effects. Workers may swing a painted screen in place to provide a new setting. Sometimes workers operate ropes and pulleys to lower an actor onto the stage.

Some plays have violent plots, but you don't see much of the action. Instead, the chorus or a messenger will give the audience a description of what has happened. Sometimes actors push a platform on rollers that bears a still scene of a murdered person or persons. The Greeks aren't worried about realism. They feel that the poetry and emotion of the words and the beauty of the movement make a play great.

WHERE TO FIND
SPORTS & RECREATION

A terra-cotta (baked clay) statue shows Greek girls playing a game called knucklebone.

GAMES

You won't find many complicated games or elaborate toys here. Greek children play with hoops, spinning tops, hobbyhorses, and miniature oxcarts or horse-drawn wagons. If someone asks you to play "Bronze Fly," go ahead and give it a try. It's a game in which a blindfolded person tries to catch another player. Another game involves two teams, each one trying to catch the other.

Dice, checkers, and ball games are all popular with children. Kids here blow up a pig's bladder to make a ball. They heat it over the ashes of a fire to make it rounder. You will also find clay dolls with arms and legs that are jointed to allow them to be moved. A popular game you may run across is knucklebone, which is played mainly by girls and women. Each playing piece is a bone with four sides of varying shapes. Each side has a point value (like dice). Players toss the bones in the air and try to catch them on the back of their hands.

SPORTS

The locals view athletics as a way to strive for physical perfection, build character, and (most importantly) worship the gods. Most athletic competitions are part of religious festivals dedicated to a god. The Olympic Games, for example, are held in honor of Zeus.

Locals favor individual contests over team competitions. Popular sports in ancient Greece include running, horse racing, chariot racing, boxing,

wrestling, discus, javelin, and long jump.

Rich people race horses. Walking is also very popular, but before you agree to join people on a walk, ask where they are headed. Locals think nothing of strolling to the Piraeus (the port five miles away from Athens) and back again.

IMPORTANT
Safety Tip

At public baths, be sure to have someone watch your clothes. Stealing clothing from dressing rooms is a big business here.

Make sure to see one of the toughest sports ever invented—the *pankration*. But participate at your own risk. It is a knock-down, drag-out, take-no-prisoners combination of boxing and wrestling. Any means of crushing an opponent is permitted except for biting or gouging out eyes. Sometimes men die. One man allowed himself to be strangled to death rather than lift his finger to indicate defeat. These folks take their sports SERIOUSLY.

Wrestling is another tough sport here. Punching is forbidden, but strangleholds, shoulder throws, and breaking an opponent's finger are perfectly acceptable. Wrestlers, like other athletes, compete naked and are usually slicked down with olive oil, which makes for a lively, if slippery, contest.

Looking for exercise? Head to the local public gymnasium, which is a prominent feature in every Greek city. Some locals call the *gymnasia* "the *palestra*," which means "place where you wrestle." But you can also just sit and chat with philosophers, professors, and others. Wealthy men often hang out at the gymnasium. They pass the time socializing and exercising.

(Facing page) *A relief from the base of a statue shows Greek wrestlers practicing their sport.*

Before you leave the gymnasium, a slave will spread oil over your body and scrape away grease and dirt with an instrument called a strigil. Then you'll be doused with cold water from a pitcher or take a plunge in a pool of chilly water.

Hot Hint

Women are excluded from the Olympics. But women race nearby as part of a festival in honor of the goddess Hera, wife of Zeus and goddess of marriage. Bet on the Spartan women *(above)*—the rigorous athletic training for girls in Sparta gives them an advantage.

THE OLYMPICS

If you visit around 500 B.C., you will find fifty or so major athletic events held at regular intervals. The most famous of Greece's athletic events is the Olympic Festival.

The official prizes are usually nothing more than a wreath of laurel, wild celery, or wild olive leaves. However, in their home city-states,

Olympic winners receive many rewards. Sculptors may create statues in their honor. Winners might receive parades, poems recited in public places, front-row seats to all public events, free meals, or cash. Winners may also receive positions of power such as political or military office.

The Olympic Festival is a religious event held every four years in honor of the god Zeus. If you visit ancient Greece during a war, you'll find that the Olympic Festival is one of the safest places to be. In all the major cities of mainland Greece, heralds announce the Olympic Truce. During the Olympic Games, Olympia is considered to be a peace zone. Even during the Peloponnesian War, visitors from enemy cities sit side-by-side to watch the events.

The event is open to all male, freeborn Greeks. Be prepared—the crowds of spectators are huge. In addition, the Olympic Games draw beggars, hucksters, fortune-tellers, and profiteers of all kinds. Artists, poets, historians, and professors give lectures there. You'll find wooden booths with horse dealers, people selling wine and food, and sellers of amulets (charms). At night, everyone in the huge crowd feasts.

One of the most exciting events is the horse-chariot race. Dozens of four-horse chariots race back and forth between two stone posts in the

Metalsmiths have decorated this bronze sword belt with a scene from a four-horse chariot race.

ground for twelve laps, a total distance of almost nine miles. Swinging galloping horses and a cart around a stone post isn't easy—the chariots can skid wildly in a dizzying dust storm of collisions, spills, and flips. This increases its appeal, at least for spectators. Few competitors even finish the race. In a chariot race during the Pythian games of 482 B.C., the winning chariot finished alone in a starting field of forty-one vehicles!

Ancient Greeks hold three other major events—Delphi, in honor of the god Apollo; Isthmia, in honor of Poseidon; and Nemea, in honor of Zeus. Along with the Olympic Games, the four events are known as a "circuit" because athletes travel from place to place to take part in them all. At Delphi, Isthmia, and Nemea, people compete in athletics, singing contests, and in playing the lyre and the flute.

WHERE TO STAY

Ruins of an ancient Greek town show the remains of narrow streets.

PRIVATE HOMES

A common local custom is for private citizens to accommodate travelers. Some home owners build special apartments to host strangers. To the invitation, "Enter!" or "I invite you to my hospitality," you should answer, "I accept." If you use this sort of accommodation and plan a long stay, you should provide your own food (with a servant or slave to cook it) and invite the host to share with you. On leaving, you and the host will exchange presents. A signet ring is a good choice.

You might be surprised to find the homes look kind of bare. Greeks don't pay much attention to their houses—they spend most of their time outdoors. Appearances are less important than simply keeping out the glare of the sun and the dust of the streets. The locals also don't want to insult the gods. While temples are elegant buildings with elaborate porticoes, ornate sculptures, and massive columns, private homes are purposely modest.

In the city, small houses huddle close together or even share common walls. A poor person's house may have only one room. Larger homes center around an open courtyard with tiny rooms arranged around it. Sun-dried mud bricks make up the walls, which have a few high, tiny windows. Mats and woolen rugs cover floors of simple beaten earth. The women of the house weave colorful hangings to brighten the walls. Doors inside homes are rare.

Ancient Greeks invented the art of mosaics, which are pictures made from small pieces of stone or glass. You probably won't see elaborate mosaics in a private house, although the *andron* (men's quarters) of a rich

Detailed mosaics cover the floors of some structures in ancient Greece.

Ceremonial bathing is also an important part of ancient Greek culture.

Greek household may have pebble mosaic floors. To make the floors, artisans lay colored river pebbles in designs, using basic shapes such as triangles, circles, and squares.

You'll notice that the rooms look almost empty. The Greeks use little furniture. Most houses have a few chairs, stools, benches, small tables, and dining couches that can double as beds. The locals often hang pots and other possessions on the walls. Women keep their personal possessions, such as jewelry and cosmetics, in baskets and small boxes.

One room you won't spot is a bathroom—at least, not the kind of bathroom you would expect. In most homes, female servants or slaves fetch water each day from a well or public fountain. A poor woman with no slave does it herself. A woman carries back water in a jar on her head. These water sources might not be nearby—sometimes they're even outside the city walls. For this reason, the ancient Greeks value water highly.

Lamps or water jars could rest in convenient niches above each bath.

Hot Hint

Male travelers might prefer a trip to the public baths *(above)*, which are convenient and reasonably priced. You can get a plunge in a tub followed by cold water poured over your head and shoulders, a cleansing substances application, oil rubbing, and strigil scraping—all for two chalci (less than one cent).

Use water sparingly. If you decide to take a bath, don't count on having a lot of privacy. You will sit in a small clay tub while a servant or slave pours cold water over you.

As for other bathroom conveniences, the large pot you see in the bathroom is the toilet. But don't expect the pot to be empty when you use it. A slave will empty it from time to time into a gutter outside (or right into the street).

PUBLIC ACCOMMODATIONS

Inns are easy to find in major cities and along important roads. Both men and women, usually metics, work as innkeepers. The inns vary in cleanliness, food quality, and comfort level, so it pays to shop around. Innkeepers might make their facilities more appealing by offering amusements, such as dice, cockfights (battles between roosters), jugglers, tightrope dancers, marionettes, and wild animals (especially monkeys). Be careful—some innkeepers try to cheat you when it's time to pay.

If you don't have enough money for an inn and can't find a local who will put you up, look for *lesche,* large public shelters in most cities. Lesche are little more than a roof over your head.

Temporary shelters are offered during national festivals. There's never enough room to accommodate the thousands of spectators. Many end up sleeping under porticoes, on temple porches, or out in the open. The wealthy bring tents and a staff of servants to keep them comfortable.

WHAT TO EAT

MEALTIMES

Few ancient Greeks eat much for *akratisma,* or breakfast. Don't be surprised to see locals dip a bit of bread, barley cake, or a roll into wine and eat a few figs for akratisma. A little before noon, when the morning's work is done, it's time for *ariston,* or lunch. Another light meal, ariston is usually wine or water, dried figs, olives, and perhaps some cheese and salted fish.

The locals eat *deipnon* (dinner), the day's most elaborate meal, around sunset. Slaves serve the food on light three-legged tables called *trapezai.* When there are no guests, men and women dine together. Wealthy men

According to ancient Greek custom, men recline on a couch while eating.

recline on a couch to eat, while women sit upright on chairs. Wives stay in the women's quarters when men entertain guests.

The Greeks don't eat with forks, so use your fingers. A carver will have already cut up your food. When you eat thick soup, use pieces of bread to scoop it out. After you eat soup off the bread, throw the bread on the floor.

There are no napkins either, so wipe your hands with bits of bread, then throw them on the floor, too. What dogs don't eat, slaves will sweep up later.

Thirsty? Ask for water or milk (from sheep or goats). You won't find tea, coffee, cocoa, orange juice, or soda. Water varies in flavor and freshness but is generally available. Wine is the standard drink for adults.

HOLD THE KETCHUP, HOLD THE MAYO

The basic foods of ancient Greece are olive oil, fish, goat cheese, flat bread, and wine. You'd better like these foods because you'll be eating them a lot!

Olives are an essential crop in ancient Greece. Although locals do eat them whole, they use most of the olives to make oil. Greeks use olive oil in place of butter for frying and to add flavor to food. In fact, you will

FOOD TO TRY

- Pork from a pig that has died of overeating (it's regarded as a great delicacy)
- Geese fattened with moistened grain
- Eggs from the rare peahen (female peacock), which rich people breed in their gardens
- *Kykeon,* a dish made from barley meal, wine, grated cheese, and sometimes honey
- Hot sausages sold by street vendors

often find a flask of olive oil on the table (it's not as good as ketchup on French fries, but the Greeks don't have potatoes anyway).

The ancient Greeks enjoy strong flavors. Your food may be seasoned with mustard, garlic, onions, and herbs such as pennyroyal, marjoram, thyme, bay leaves, and mint. By the way, the locals eat garlic in astonishing quantities (unfortunately, breath mints haven't been invented yet). You'll find salt but no pepper or other spices.

If you enjoy sweets, your choices may be limited. Sugar is unknown here. No sugar means no candies or puddings. But be sure to try some delicious honey from mountain farms, where beekeeping is common.

A musician plays a flute as four women knead bread dough.

Fishers in ancient Greece use nets and fishing poles to catch fish.

The locals eat bread at every meal. Bakers sell many different kinds of bread and rolls, and many people prepare bread at home. Cooks use barley meal or wheat flour to make dough, which they form into large flat loaves to cook on a griddle or to bake in circular, domed ovens. You may even find flat breads used as plates. It's perfectly okay to eat the food on the plate and then eat the plate itself.

The waters around Greece teem with fish, so there's plenty of seafood. Buy fresh fish from the fishmonger in the agora or even from fishermen unloading their catch at the harbor.

FOODS TO TRY, at your own risk

- Spartan black broth (made from pork broth, blood, vinegar, and salt). A visitor who tasted it said that he now understands why no Spartan fears death.

- A dish (unnamed) made from milk, eggs, flour, brains, fresh cheese, and honey, all cooked in rich broth and wrapped up in a fig leaf

- Black pudding (blood and fat stuffed into an animal's bladder, then roasted)

DINING ON A BUDGET

What you eat in ancient Greece will depend largely on what you spend. The contrast between the foods available to the rich and the poor is particularly obvious during the height of Athens's power (479–431 B.C.).

If your budget is limited, you'll have to be satisfied with a simple barley cake or some porridge. You may be able to buy a few dried figs or find a leaf of lettuce or a sprig of thyme growing wild on the hills.

If you can spend a little more, you can eat like the working class and dine on broth and barley-meal porridge, gruel, or bread, plus a handful of olives, a few figs, eggs, and some goat's milk cheese. Occasionally you'll be able to afford some salted fish. Peas and beans are tasty raw or cooked with oil, vinegar, and honey. You can buy cheap pea soup from vendors in the street.

After this bull is sacrificed, worshipers eat part of the meat and leave part for the gods.

Try to avoid visiting during one of the many famines (food shortages) that hit ancient Greece. The mountainous landscape means that there aren't many flat fields for growing crops. And heavy winter rains wash from the soil the nutrients plants need for food. The locals haven't discovered crop rotation (moving crops each year to let the soil rest), so the land tends to wear out quickly. Although the ancient Greeks do import food from other areas (the best fish reportedly comes from the Black Sea region), shortages occur periodically.

WHERE'S THE BEEF?

If you have plenty to spend, you may also enjoy (as the rich folks do) goat, mutton, pork, or game such as deer, hare, partridge, and thrush (small birds) in addition to the standard sorts of foods. But meat (especially beef) is expensive and is a rare treat for most city-dwellers in ancient Greece. A public sacrifice is generally the only place where the poor (and tourists) can get meat. On these occasions, priests kill a cow, pig, sheep, or goat. They set aside some of the meat for the god (usually the worst parts, such as the inedible organs and bones). People roast the rest of the animal on a spit over an open fire, then distribute it to the crowd.

In the countryside, people eat meat more often. You'll find exotic choices such as wild boar, quail, wild duck, goose, partridge, and blackbird. Rural Greeks keep pigs and chickens to provide food for dinner parties. But you'll mostly see goats, which give milk that locals drink as well as make into cheese. Goats also provide meat and skins that people can tan into leather.

WHERE TO FIND SOUVENIRS

Fresh tuna is for sale in agoras across ancient Greece.

THE AGORA

The agoras are marketplaces where you can buy or trade anything from fish to philosophy. This is definitely where the mall life is. Listen for the crier, who will ring a bell when the market opens. Believe it or not, agoras are off-limits to people who avoid military service, disgrace themselves in battle, or mistreat their parents!

On business days, an agora fills with wicker market stalls, grouped into rings according to products. There are rings for perfume, money changing, pickled fish, and slaves. At first you may be overwhelmed by noise. Pigs squeal, poultry cackles. Criers walk up and down the agora, calling out that someone has a horse to sell or that someone has lost a valuable ring and will pay a reward to the finder. Add to this the hollers of "Buy my oil" and "Buy my cheese." Workers hammer and clank in the workshops near the agora. The price of items in the market is rarely firm, so be sure to bargain. The locals haggle in loud angry voices—you can do the same.

At Athens's Agora, the fishmonger rings a bell to announce the arrival of fresh fish, straight from the harbor. This is followed by a stampede of customers who elbow each other and call out their requests. Next you'll hear heated arguments. The fishmonger is notorious for his ability to get the highest price.

If you need shoes, look to the southwest corner and you'll see a round building. This is the Tholos, where the Council's executive committee meets. Next to the Tholos is the shop of Simon the cobbler (shoemaker), who also sells iron hobnails and bone eyelets, should you need any. To make a pair of sandals, Simon will place each of your feet on the leather and cut around them to make the soles. His sandals are a good buy and are sure to fit!

TAKE IT from a Local

You will find everything sold together in the same place at Athens: figs, witnesses to summonses, bunches of grapes, turnips, pears, apples, givers of evidence, roses, medlars, porridge, honeycombs, chickpeas, lawsuits, beestings-puddings, myrtle, allotment machines, irises, lambs, water clocks, laws, indictments.
—*Comic poet Eubulus*

This shopper inspects a piece of pottery before he buys.

The Agora really is a great place to hang out, which is basically what the local folks do there. They trade, vote, argue, meet friends, buy provisions, and gossip. In Athens important people such as Socrates, Pericles, Aristophanes, and Plato sit under the shade of the trees or stroll through the porticoes that line the square. They exchange ideas among the stalls of figs, turnips, and flowers.

You'll notice that rich Athenians carry their money in purses. Poor folks keep coins in their mouths. When they want to buy something, they pluck the money from between their cheek and gums. (You may have to dry your change!)

THE CERAMICUS

Pottery is everywhere in ancient Greece. Most things are stored in pottery jars, since there is no cardboard or plastic to make containers. The ancient Greeks use pottery to make storage jars, drinking cups, vases, mixing bowls, plates, and other containers. To buy pottery in Athens, go to the Ceramicus (potters' quarter). That's where craftspeople sell their pieces to the public. Most of the artisans live nearby.

The high-quality clay turns a beautiful reddish-brown color when fired (baked at a high temperature). Artists paint elaborate scenes on the clay before firing it.

Early potters chose decorative or geometric designs, but if you visit after 600 B.C. you will find fantastic scenes of gods and heroes in action. Other items show farming, seafaring, and daily life. In the 500s B.C. in Athens, artisans make black-figure pottery. They color the skin of the male figures black and the women's skin white. They make cuts in the clay to help create detail and fine lines.

After 520 B.C., you will find red-figure pottery all the rage. The artisans paint the backgrounds black, leaving outlined human and animal figures open to the clay's red color. A popular Athenian style of the 400s B.C. is the white-ground technique in which figures are drawn in black against a white background. Potters use this style for *lekythoi,* pitchers that the locals leave as offerings in tombs.

SCULPTURE

It's probably not something you'll lug home, but check out the sculpture in ancient Greece. Patrons hire artisans to make specific pieces of sculpture. And since Greek sculptors expect their work to be seen in public places, particularly temples, they make sure that the objects appear worthy of the gods.

You'll be surprised to see that a statue's skin, hair, clothing, and other features are painted in vivid colors. Workers use bronze to make armor and horse trappings. The statue of Zeus at Olympia wears sandals and a robe made from real gold. Walls, columns, and other parts of temples are painted in bright colors, which makes the sculptures look especially dramatic.

Look for sculptures by Phidias, one of the greatest sculptors of all time. He designed the figures that line the top of the Parthenon. (He may not have carved them, but he directed the project and made the clay models for the figures.) If you want to see what Phidias did while others finished the figures for the top of the Parthenon, step inside. Gaze upon his statue of Athena, which stands over thirty feet high.

How to Stay Safe & Healthy

A physician treats a patient's wounded shoulder in this relief.

Take Two Bowls of Gruel & Call Me in the Morning

In ancient Greece, *iatroi* (physicians) do epidemics, which means that they travel to towns across the region. *Epidemics* means "visits to places." But each *iatros* also has a workplace (called the *iatreion*) in town. You'll most likely find an iatreion in an open shop in the front of a house near the town's agora.

The iatreion will be roomy and well lit by windows and oil lamps. The iatros keeps the room equipped with surgical instruments, drugs, and scrolls of medical literature. The first thing you will notice, however, is the odor—a combination of smoke from the fire, where tools are kept red-hot for cauterizing (burning) wounds. You'll also notice fumes from boiling drugs, aromas from herbs, resins, and spices on the shelves, and the scent of burned flesh.

Depending upon your complaint, the iatros may use medications or procedures such as bleeding, blistering, or severely restricting the diet. He might even try to cause vomiting or diarrhea. If you have a stubborn problem, the iatros might bleed you from the arm, make you vomit, and put you on a starvation diet of thin barley gruel and oxymel (a mixture containing water, vinegar, and a little honey).

If all else fails, you can do what the locals do—visit the temple of Asclepius, god of medicine. Relax on the holy grounds, listen to hymns and wait for nightfall. Then lie down to sleep in the sacred hall (called the *abaton*) and wait for the god to appear in a dream and give you advice. The priests will assist by receiving a gift for the god (a candle

TAKE IT from a Local

With regard to the gangrene of fleshy parts . . . when the forearm and leg drop off, the patients readily recover. Those parts of the body which are below the boundaries of the blackening are to be removed at the joint, as soon as they are completely dead and have lost their sensibility; care being taken not to wound any living part . . . Such cases . . . are more formidable to look at than to treat.

—*"On Joints," from the* Hippocratic Collection

An ancient Greek left this ex-voto (offering) to thank Asclepius for a cured leg.

will do) and recording the results of your visit. The locals believe that if you dream that the god cures you, you will become well.

There are at least one hundred temples of Asclepius, so you should be able to find one nearby no matter where you stay. Grateful patients leave behind ex-votos, (thanks offerings). A good choice is a model of the healed body part (a leg, for example). You will see the models hanging on the walls of the temples as advertisements for new patients.

LOCAL DISEASES & DANGERS

Watch out for disease here. Malaria is common in the Athens area during the fifth century B.C. You may also run into measles, tetanus, anthrax, and smallpox. Injuries, such as being pierced by an arrow, are a common problem during periods of war (there are a lot of those in this era). The only anesthetics are opium and the root of mandrake (a powerful herb), and neither works very well. Doctors sew up wounds using a thread and a bronze needle.

The iatros may create a tricky and exotic bandage. Many iatroi pride themselves on these elaborate designs, which involve wrapping the bandage into an impressive ornament.

You should avoid getting hit or kicked in the head. The Greeks worry about dents in the skull that don't produce a fracture (crack) because they are afraid the blood and pus will have no way out. To find out whether the skull has actually been fractured, the iatros will shave your head, enlarge the wound, lift the scalp all around it, and pack the space with lint. Then he will plug the wound with a plaster made from boiling vinegar and barley flour. He'll cover the whole thing with a bandage. The next day, he will remove everything, smear your skull with a paint that looks like black shoe polish, and then cover it again with oil,

77

linen, and more barley plaster. On the third day, he will scrape your skull, removing the black paint with a sharp knife. The black paint will have seeped into the indentations in the skull, highlighting any cracks. If the iatros finds a fracture, he'll leave it to heal on its own. But if he finds no hole or crack, he will make one by drilling slowly into your skull (drilling too fast burns the bone).

Ancient Greek doctors wash wounds with vinegar or wine. While both of these sting, they have germ-fighting qualities that help prevent infection. And you do NOT want an infection, as there are no antibiotics (medicines that attack infection-causing bacteria). Doctors do use advanced techniques, such as auscultation (listening to the chest for sounds), the tourniquet (a device for squeezing major arteries or vessels to stop massive bleeding), and surgical drains (pieces of tin pipe that allow pus or blood to leave the body).

WARS, CATASTROPHES, & OTHER ANNOYANCES

Plague Avoid visiting Athens in 430 B.C., when the plague arrives. At least one-third and possibly as many as two-thirds of the population will be wiped out in a single year. By 426 B.C., the epidemic will be over.

The plague attacks rich and poor, young and old, local and visitor. Don't take it lightly. It may be typhus, smallpox, or a deadly form of scarlet fever. Greek doctors have no successful treatments to offer, and many of them die as well. People abandon bodies in temples and streets, where

Back TO THE FUTURE

In the 1990s, archaeologists unearthed a mass grave in Athens containing nearly one thousand bodies—probably plague victims. The bodies may hold clues about the cause of the terrible plague.

A Greek soldier (right) *fights a mounted Persian attacker* (left).

officials collect them for quick burial. Things get so hectic that workers toss many bodies into common graves.

Watch for Wars In 490 and 480–479 B.C., mainland Greece will be invaded by the Persian Empire. Persia encompasses about one million square miles and is the greatest empire the world has yet seen. The Greeks unite to defeat the Persians but not without tremendous effort.

City-states often battle each other. Throughout the period of 431–404 B.C., Sparta and its allies war periodically with Athens and its allies. Sparta is unbeatable on land, and Athens is supreme at sea, so battles often end in a stalemate. Without much military technology, battles often involve circling the enemy city (most are surrounded by walls) and waiting for its defenders to starve, give up, or be betrayed.

The skirmishing comes to a head in 404 B.C. in what the locals call "the war between the Peloponnesians and the Athenians." In modern times, it is known as the Peloponnesian War. Sparta and its allies defeat Athens and its allies, ending Athens's seventy-five-year reign as the richest and most powerful Greek city-state.

LAW & ORDER

The streets of Athens and other cities in ancient Greece are generally safe. But there are some dangers, especially after dark. That's when thugs may lurk in dark alleys to club and rob unsuspecting walkers. Watch out for members of "the Rips" or "the Independents," gangs of young men who attack innocent folks at night.

Handy WORDS & PHRASES

Some Greek soldiers are referred to as hoplites *(above),* named after the round bronze shield called a *hoplon* used by the soldiers. Large groups of hoplites advance in rectangular formation, carrying eight-foot spears. This unit, called a phalanx, attempts to break through enemy ranks.

A Scythian policeman in traditional uniform blows a trumpet.

The locals consider the idea of one citizen policing another distasteful, so foreigners and slaves maintain order. Some police are Scythian tribesmen from the north. They can be recognized by their long trousers and high-peaked, tight-fitting caps. They keep order in public places such as the Agora in Athens. They patrol the town at night and make arrests. Look for their station on the hill of Areopagus, near the Acropolis.

Athens relies on its citizens to detect and prosecute crimes. Any citizen who sees a crime can take the wrongdoer to an official. If the official arrests the offender, the person who accused him gets half of the fine a criminal must pay.

If a citizen wants justice, he must take the case to court himself. Ordinary people handle cases of theft, murder, high treason, and other serious crimes. It is a rare citizen who is not involved in a legal action every few years or so. And when cases involve important issues or well-known people, spectators crowd behind a railing that separates them from the participants.

Juries numbering 201, 401, or more decide cases. Until the day of the trial, no one knows who will be on the jury. (You don't have to worry about being picked, however. Only citizens can serve on juries.) Each juror has a token such as a pebble or shell to place in one of two jars—one to condemn, the other to acquit (free).

Ancient Greeks don't like the idea of imprisonment. Instead, convicted criminals face fines, lose the right to vote, or are put to death.

The *kleroterion* is a machine for selecting jurors. It consists of a box with rows and columns of slots. The names of eligible citizens are placed in the slots, and then black and white balls are mixed in a hopper. As the balls come out of a tube one at a time, the color determines whether that row of candidates is selected (white) or excused (black).

Criminals receive the death sentence for crimes such as murder, theft, picking pockets, housebreaking, kidnapping, treason, and temple robbing. Officials force them to drink a dose of hemlock (a poison), which causes paralysis and then death.

During the 400s B.C., Athenians use ostracism (temporarily banishing someone) to rid the city of people who appear to be dangerous but who aren't criminals. Athenians can vote to banish any citizen for ten years. Ostracism is designed to protect the city-state against wealthy politicians who try to seize power.

The various city-states develop their own systems of law. Ancient Greeks particularly respect cities on the island of Crete, such as Dreros, for their laws. Dreros has a written code of laws as early as the seventh century B.C.

WHO'S WHO IN ANCIENT GREECE

ANAXIMANDER

Anaximander (ca. 601–545 B.C.) is a brilliant scientist and philosopher. He authors a history of the natural world, which includes the first Greek map of the heavens and earth. The map also describes the movement of the constellations. His book emphasizes science over myth in explaining the universe. He guesses at the law of gravity, wonders about evolution, and figures out that basic matter isn't really destroyed but instead undergoes change. In his spare time, Anaximander constructs the first sundial in the Greek world. He also creates a model that is an ancestor of the modern planetarium.

ASPASIA

Aspasia lives in the middle of the fifth century B.C. She comes from Miletus in Asia Minor, but she settles in Athens as a metic. Her speaking skills are well respected, and powerful men seek her out for advice. One of her admirers is Socrates. Like him, Aspasia is criticized for challenging accepted ideas.

HIPPOCRATES

Hippocrates (ca. 460–377 B.C.) is a highly respected doctor who is remembered as the founder of scientific medicine. He teaches that medical practice should be based on observation rather than theory. You may find him at Cos, an island off the coast of Asia Minor, where his school of medicine is well known among the locals. Hippocrates writes fifty-three scientific books on medical topics.

Back TO THE FUTURE

Modern-day doctors still take the Hippocratic Oath, a pledge attributed to Hippocrates, when they first begin to practice medicine. The oath describes medical ethics and is based on Hippocrates' idea of the ideal doctor.

PERICLES

Pericles (ca. 494–429 B.C.) is definitely the man in Athens. A powerful speaker, he is elected *strategos* (one of ten top military commanders) year after year from 443 to 429 B.C. His democratic reforms and public works transform the city. He is looked up to as a brilliant leader and is credited with turning Athens into a powerful force.

PLATO

Plato (ca. 427–347 B.C.), an Athenian philosopher, is one of history's most influential thinkers. Plato imagines a society where slavery is abolished and women are equal citizens. His Academy (one of the world's first important institutions of higher learning) will shape the course of philosophy for the next thousand years. He records in writing the thoughts of Socrates, who was his teacher.

SOCRATES

Socrates (469–399 B.C.) is a great thinker and teacher. In his style of debate, he often pretends to be ignorant of a topic to allow an opponent to unintentionally destroy his or her own argument. His unusual approach to education gets him into trouble, and his refusal to compromise his beliefs will result in his death. According to Plato, Socrates said, "I am not going to alter my conduct, not even if I have to die a hundred deaths." Accused of corrupting the minds of young people and of showing disrespect to the gods, he will be imprisoned then forced to take his own life by drinking hemlock.

Preparing for the Trip

Make Your Own Mosaic

Decorate a wall in your room with this simple-to-make mosaic!
You will need:

> colored construction paper
> pencil
> scissors
> glue

Choose a piece of construction paper as a background. Try a dark color, such as blue or black. Cut several different colors of construction paper into one-and-a-half-inch-wide strips. Next, cut the strips into one-and-a-half-inch squares and triangles.

Draw a simple figure such as a flower, bird, fish, butterfly, or animal on the paper you'll use as the background. Place your tiles on the paper inside the outline of the figure you've drawn. Place them close to one another but not touching. Use different colors to show different parts of the figure. For example, if you choose to draw a butterfly, try using different colors for the body and the wings. Be creative! Be sure to leave small cracks between the tiles so that the background color shows through.

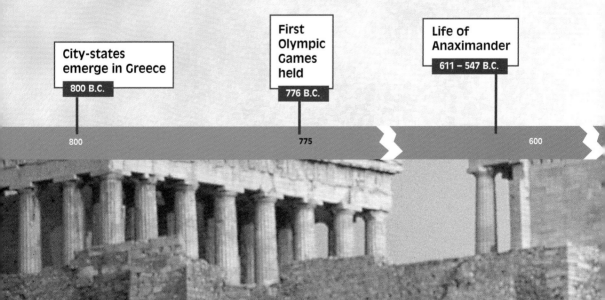

City-states
emerge in Greece
800 B.C.

First
Olympic
Games
held
776 B.C.

Life of
Anaximander
611 – 547 B.C.

800

775

600

Now that you have arranged the tiles, glue them into place by carefully picking up each one, dabbing some glue on the back, and then setting it back in place. When you are done gluing down the figure, fill in the background of your mosaic with one shade of tiles. Try not to use a color that you have used in your design. Try edging the mosaic with a colorful, geometric border!

HAVE YOUR OWN OLYMPICS!

Have you ever wanted to compete in the Olympics? Organize your own! Ask a group of friends to compete in races and games at recess or after school every day for one week. At the end of the week, crown the winners with homemade wreaths. You will need:

> green construction paper
> scissors
> stapler or glue

To make the wreaths, cut leaf shapes from green construction paper. Then staple or glue the leaves onto a long strip of construction paper to form a wreath that fits on your head.

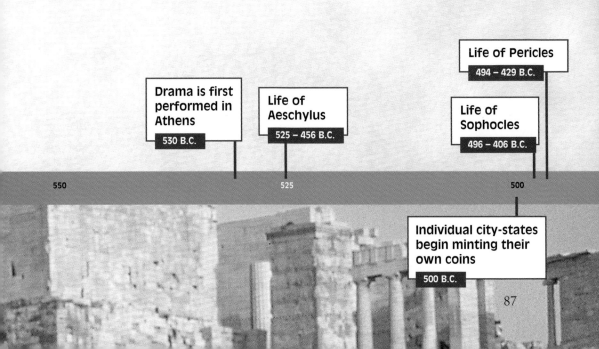

Life of Pericles
494 – 429 B.C.

Drama is first performed in Athens
530 B.C.

Life of Aeschylus
525 – 456 B.C.

Life of Sophocles
496 – 406 B.C.

550

525

500

Individual city-states begin minting their own coins
500 B.C.

GLOSSARY

agora: An ancient Greek marketplace

citizen: A resident of an ancient Greek city-state who has full rights and responsibilities. Only adult males born in the city-state can be citizens.

city-state: A self-governing region, usually an urban area and surrounding farmland

helot: A Spartan farmworker with little freedom. Helots worked on land owned by wealthy Spartans.

iatros: A doctor in ancient Greece

metic: A foreigner who is a long-term resident of a Greek city-state. A metic cannot be a citizen nor can the children of a metic.

oracle: Someone who foretells the future

ostracism: A temporary banishment. Greek leaders are ostracized if others feel that the leader has gained too much power.

peninsula: A stretch of land almost completely surrounded by water

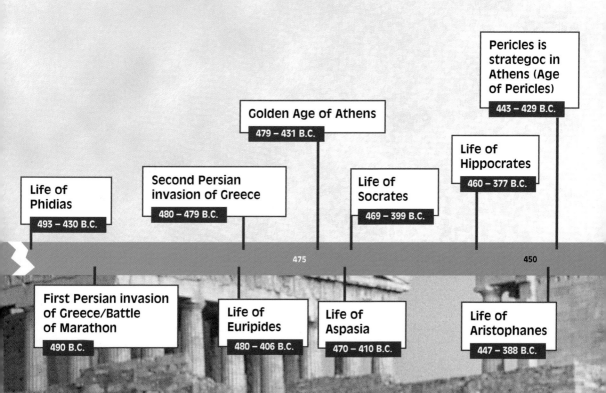

Pericles is strategoc in Athens (Age of Pericles)
443 – 429 B.C.

Golden Age of Athens
479 – 431 B.C.

Life of Hippocrates
460 – 377 B.C.

Life of Phidias
493 – 430 B.C.

Second Persian invasion of Greece
480 – 479 B.C.

Life of Socrates
469 – 399 B.C.

475

450

First Persian invasion of Greece/Battle of Marathon
490 B.C.

Life of Euripides
480 – 406 B.C.

Life of Aspasia
470 – 410 B.C.

Life of Aristophanes
447 – 388 B.C.

Pronunciation Guide

Acropolis	uh-KRAH-puh-lihs
Aegean	ih-JEE-uhn
Aesclepius	ehs-KLEE-pee-uhs
agora	AH-gohr-uh
Anaximander	uh-NAK-sih-MAN-dur
Aristophanes	ahr-uh-STAH-fuh-neez
Aristotle	AHR-ih-stah-tuhl
Aspasia	uhs-PAY-zhuh
Delphi	DEHL-fy
Demosthenes	dih-MAHS-thuh-neez
Euripides	yoo-RIH-puh-deez
Hippocrates	hih-PAH-kruh-teez
iatros	ee-uh-TROHS
metic	MEH-tihk
obol	OH-buhl
Panathenaic	pan-uh-thuh-NAY-ihk
Parthenon	PAHR-thuh-nahn
Peloponnesus	peh-luh-puh-NEE-suhs
Pericles	PEHR-uh-kleez
Phidias	FIH-dee-uhs
Plato	PLAY-toh
Socrates	SAH-kruh-teez

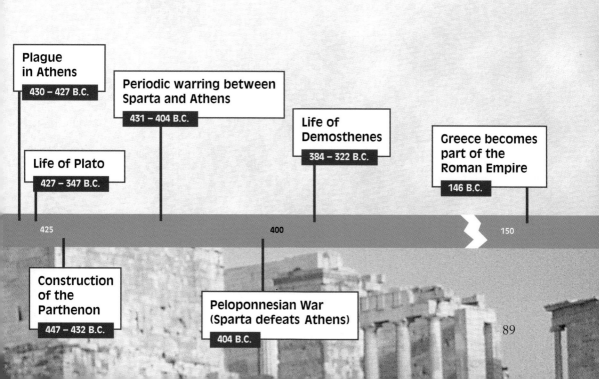

Plague in Athens
430 – 427 B.C.

Periodic warring between Sparta and Athens
431 – 404 B.C.

Life of Demosthenes
384 – 322 B.C.

Greece becomes part of the Roman Empire
146 B.C.

Life of Plato
427 – 347 B.C.

425

400

150

Construction of the Parthenon
447 – 432 B.C.

Peloponnesian War (Sparta defeats Athens)
404 B.C.

89

FURTHER READING

Dazzling! Jewelry of the Ancient World. Buried Worlds Series. Minneapolis: Runestone Press, 1994.

Glowacki, Kevin T., and Nancy L. Klein. *The Ancient City of Athens*. 1998. <http://www.indiana.edu/~kglowack/athens> (n.d.).

Gonen, Rivka. *Fired Up! Making Pottery in Ancient Times*. Buried Worlds Series. Minneapolis: Runestone Press, 1993.

Hamilton, Edith. *The Greek Way*. New York: W.W. Norton, 1942.

Kotapish, Dawn. *Daily Life in Ancient and Modern Athens*. Cities through Time Series. Minneapolis: Runestone Press, 2001.

Loverance, Rowena. *Ancient Greece*. See Through History Series. New York: Viking, 1993.

Nardo, Don. *Life in Ancient Greece*. Way People Live Series. San Diego: Lucent Books, 1996.

Pearson, Anne. *Ancient Greece*. Eyewitness Books, no. 37. New York: Alfred A. Knopf, 1992.

Pearson, Anne. *Everyday Life in Ancient Greece*. Clues to the Past Series. New York: Franklin Watts, 1994.

Sauvain, Philip. *Over Two Thousand Years Ago: In Ancient Greece*. History Detectives Series. New York: Maxwell Macmillan International, 1992.

BIBLIOGRAPHY

Adkins, Lesley, and Roy A. Adkins. *Handbook to Life in Ancient Greece*. New York: Oxford University Press, 1998.

Amos, H. D., and A. G. P. Lang. *These Were the Greeks*. Amersham, Bucks, U.K.: Hulton Educational Publications, Ltd., 1979.

Andrewes, Antony. *The Greeks*. New York: Alfred A. Knopf, 1967.

Bowra, C. M. *Classical Greece*. New York: Time-Life Books, 1971.

Cartwright, Frederick F. *Disease and History*. New York: Dorset Press, 1972.

Casson, Lionel. *Travel in the Ancient World*. Baltimore: Johns Hopkins Press, 1994.

Coolidge, Olivia. *The Golden Days of Greece*. New York: Thomas Y. Crowell, 1968.

Davis, William Stearns. *A Day in Old Athens: A Picture of Athenian Life*. New York: Biblo and Tannen, 1960.

Duby, Georges, and Philippe Ariès, eds. *A History of Private Life: From Pagan Rome to Byzantium*. Cambridge, MA: The Belknap Press of Harvard University Press, 1987.

Fitzhardinge, L. F. *The Spartans*. London: Thames and Hudson Ltd., 1980.

Flaceliere, Robert. *Daily Life in Greece at the Time of Pericles*. New York: The Macmillan Company, 1965.

Fleischman, John. "In Classical Athens, a Market Trading in the Currency of Ideas." *Smithsonian* (July 1993): 38–42.

Freeman, Charles. *Egypt, Greece and Rome: Civilizations of the Ancient Mediterranean*. New York: Oxford University Press, 1996.

Garland, Robert. *Daily Life of the Ancient Greeks*. Westport, CT: Greenwood Press, 1998.

Gulick, Charles Burton. *The Life of the Ancient Greeks*. New York: D. Appleton and Company, 1902.

Hale, William Harlan, and the editors of Horizon Magazine. *The Horizon Book of Ancient Greece*. New York: American Heritage, 1965.

James, Peter, and Nick Thorpe. *Ancient Inventions*. New York: Ballantine Books, 1994.

Jenkins, Ian. *Greek and Roman Life*. Cambridge, MA: Harvard University Press, 1986.

Kagan, Donald. *Botsford and Robinson's Hellenic History*. New York: The Macmillan Company, 1969.

Leon, Vicki. *Uppity Women of Ancient Times*. Berkeley: Conari Press, 1995.

Levi, Peter. *Atlas of the Greek World*. New York: Facts on File, 1980.

Loverance, Rowena. *Ancient Greece*. New York: Viking, 1993.

Macdonald, Fiona. *How Would You Survive as an Ancient Greek?* New York: Franklin Watts, 1995.

Majno, Guido. *The Healing Hand: Man and Wound in the Ancient World*. Cambridge, MA: Harvard University Press, 1991.

Nichols, Roger, and Kenneth McLeish. *Through Greek Eyes*. Cambridge, U.K.: Cambridge University Press, 1974.

Parke, H.W. *Festivals of the Athenians*. Ithaca, NY: Cornell University Press, 1986.

Pearson, Anne. *What Do We Know about the Greeks?* New York: Peter Bedrick Books, 1992.

Quennell, Marjorie, and C. H. B. Quennell. *Everyday Things in Ancient Greece*. New York: G. P. Putnam's Sons, 1960.

Reader's Digest. *Everyday Life through the Ages*. London: Reader's Digest, 1992.

Robinson, C. E. *Everyday Life in Ancient Greece*. Oxford: The Clarendon Press, 1968.

Sacks, David. *Encyclopedia of the Ancient Greek World*. New York: Facts on File, 1995.

Silvestri, Dr. "The Civilization of Ancient Greece," *Dr. Silvestri's WWW Ancient World History Resource*. 1998. <http://ancientworld.simplenet.com/chapter8/index2.html> (n.d.).

Sweet, Waldo E. *Sport and Recreation in Ancient Greece*. New York: Oxford University Press, 1987.

Tannahill, Reay. *Food in History*. New York: Stein and Day, 1973.

Werner, Paul. *Life in Greece in Ancient Times*. Geneva, Switzerland: Minerva Press, 1986.

INDEX

Acropolis, 14–15, 17, 42, 49, 81
Aegean Sea, 11, 12
Aeschylus, 87
Agora, 17, 20, 42, 46, 47, 68, 71, 76, 81, 88
Anaximander, 83, 86
Andosthenes of Arcadia, 13
animals, 11, 21, 36, 65, 67, 69, 70, 72
Apollo, 34, 43, 58
archaeology, 7–8
architecture, 7, 9, 14–15, 16–17, 35, 42–45, 60
Aristophanes, 73, 88
Aristotle, 8, 33
art and artworks, 7, 9, 17, 22–23, 24–25, 26, 30, 31, 32, 35, 36–37, 38, 41, 45, 47, 48, 49, 50, 53, 54, 56, 57, 60–61, 64–65, 66–67, 68, 69, 71, 73–74, 75, 78, 79, 80, 83, 84, 85
Aspasia, 83, 88
Assembly, 28, 45
Athena, 17, 20, 34, 43, 48, 49, 74
Athens, 8, 9, 12, 13, 14–15, 16, 24, 28, 31, 34, 42–43, 45, 46, 48–49, 50, 55, 69, 72, 73, 78, 79–80, 81, 82, 84, 88, 89
Attica, 11, 12, 50

barley, 11, 64, 67, 68, 69, 76, 77–78
bathroom, 61–62
Boeotia, 14

calendars, 12–13
ceremonies, 35, 36, 37, 43–44
children, 13, 29–30, 31, 53–54
Chthonians, 34–35
citizens, 27, 28, 29, 45, 81, 82, 88
city-states, 14–17, 18, 19, 20, 24, 28, 29, 79–80, 82, 86, 87, 88
classes of people, 16, 29, 31, 45, 49, 55, 63, 64–65, 69, 70, 73

climate, 11–12, 24, 39, 70
clocks and sundials, 12, 13, 72, 83
clothes, 6, 38–40, 55, 72
coastline, 10–11, 24
council, 28, 29, 72
Crete, 19, 82
currency, 18, 19, 20. *See also* money.
customs, 13, 14, 27, 28, 33, 34, 40–41, 59, 73

Delphi, 24, 43, 44, 58
Delphic Oracle, 43, 44
democracy, 28–29, 84
Demosthenes, 45, 89
documents, 7, 46
drama, 33, 87

economy, 18–21, 27, 28, 30, 31–32, 70, 71–73
elections, 28, 29
Eretria, 20
Euripides, 33, 88

farming, 6–7, 11, 26, 31, 67, 70, 74
fashion and beauty, 38–41
festivals, 25, 35, 48–50, 56–58, 63. *See also* Olympic Games.
fish, 66, 68, 69, 70, 71, 72
food, 6, 21, 25, 34, 46, 57, 59, 63, 64–70, 72, 73
foreign policy, 27, 28

games, 25, 53–54, 63. *See also* Olympic Games.
geography and the land, 6–7, 9, 11, 17, 70
gods and goddesses, 17, 25, 29, 34–37, 43–44, 50, 54, 56, 57, 58, 60, 69, 70, 74, 76–77
gold, 19, 74

ABOUT THE AUTHOR

Nancy Day is the author of nine books and forty-five articles for young people. She loves to read and is fascinated with the idea of time travel, which she says is "actually history in a great disguise." Her interest in time travel inspired the Passport to History series. Nancy Day lives with her husband, son, and two cats in a house that was built in 1827—before the Civil War. She often imagines what it would be like to go back in time to meet the shipbuilder who once lived there.

Acknowledgments for Quoted Material p. 14, p. 28, p. 32, as quoted by C. M. Bowra, *Classical Greece* (New York: Time-Life Books, 1971); p. 27, Thucydides, *The History of the Peloponnesian War*, translated by Richard Crowley (New York: Dutton, 1950); p. 72, as quoted by John Fleischman, "In Classical Athens, a Market Trading in the Currency of Ideas," *Smithsonian* (July 1993, p. 41); p. 76, as quoted by Guido Majno, *The Healing Hand: Man and Wound in the Ancient World* (Cambridge: Harvard University Press, 1991).

Photo Acknowledgments
The images in this book are used with the permission of: © Erich Lessing/Art Resource, NY, pp. 2, 33, 36–37, 38, 41, 48, 66–67, 68, 69, 73, 75, 79; © Robert Fried, pp. 6–7; © James Davis; Eye Ubiquitous/Corbis, pp. 10, 60; © Jonathan Blair/Corbis, p. 13; © Kevin Schafer/Corbis, pp. 14–15; © Ronald Sheridan/ Ancient Art and Architecture Collection, Ltd., pp. 18 (rods), 19, 24–25, 31, 44, 51, 59, 77, 80, 81; James Marrinan, pp. 18 (right coins), 21 (both); The Granger Collection, pp. 18 (left coin), 20, 26, 30, 32, 53, 82; Scala/Art Resource, NY, pp. 22–23, 35, 56, 57, 71, 84 (bottom), 85 (top); TRIP/B. North, p. 42; © Archivo Iconografico, S. A./Corbis, p. 45, 61; © Stock Montage, p. 47; Nimatallah/Art Resource, NY, pp. 49, 54; © Roger Wood/Corbis, p. 62; © Mimmo Jodice/Corbis, pp. 64–65; © Alinari/Art Resource, NY, pp. 83, 84 (top); © Massimo Listri/Corbis, p. 85 (bottom); Daniel H. Condit, pp. 86–87, 88–89.

Front cover: Scala/Art Resource, NY, (both).